The Crazy Cat Lover's
Handbook

by

Stella Rheingold

Published by the Sovereign Media Group.

Thank you for purchasing this book!

You may enjoy other titles by this author:

101 fun things to do in retirement: An irreverent, outrageous and fun guide to life after work – Stella Rheingold

You may also like to join

"The Sovereign Readers Club".

As a member you will get a host of special offers, from pre release, advance copies of new titles, FREE and discount books from the publisher, as well as the chance to give feedback and interact with your favourite authors.

http://bit.ly/1jWbqDj

Click the link above for your special joining gift of a free e-copy of "Think Happy: 7 Simple Steps to a Happier Life" by Margaret Hart

INTRODUCTION

So you love a cat? Well that's not really all that surprising, cats are lovely! From their cute little noses to the tip of their furry little tails we absolutely adore them. For most of us cat lovers our kitties reign supreme! We take them into our hearts, we cuddle them, we play with them, we give them clean washing to sleep on and expensive furniture on which to sharpen their claws; and most importantly of all we feed them.

Some people however mistakenly believe that they own their cats. Let me assure you, these people are completely deluded!

What's really going on with these delusional, self-described cat "owners", is that they have unwittingly entered themselves into indentured servitude and whether they realize it or not their life is no longer their own. To these poor hapless souls I say this, "Wake up people! Your cat owns you!"

Once you have been drafted into royal service, escape is not possible. You now live to serve your feline masters, and there are strict rules and protocols that must be observed.

As most of us are quite aware, working for a supreme being has its challenges. Cats can be demanding taskmasters and we are only human after all. Seriously, who among us hasn't felt the sting of a feline death stare when we got Mr Fluffypants's telepathically transmitted dinner order wrong, AGAIN!

Fortunately help is at hand, literally! You have in your hand a handbook, a comprehensive guide to pleasing your furry feline overlord.

While some of the lessons contained herein may seem simple at first, they can take years to master. But have confidence my friends, if you are conscientious in your studies and practice daily you will no doubt rise through the ranks, from novice to initiate to adept, right up to coveted titles of master and grandmaster. Some of you may even reach the exalted status of "preferred lap".

While I will frequently refer to "your" cat throughout the text, please understand this does not imply that you own your cat in anyway. It is meant in the same way as one might say "your king" or "your boss". As it is with your boss or your king, you don't own your cat, your cat rules you!

THE GROUND RULES

Get your priorities sorted

When choosing to dedicate your life to the care of a feline there are certain ground rules that humans should observe in order to maintain a good working relationship.

To start with, no matter what you are doing it is not as important as giving your cat your full attention. This can be very difficult for people who are still in the novice stage. Cats have mastered the art of being in the present moment. There is now and there is NOW! Later is simply too abstract a concept to be entertained. But it is exactly the same as it is in any other service industry. The needs of the client (or cat) take precedence and all other tasks must be deferred until the client (cat) is totally satisfied.

ACQUIRING A FELINE OVERLORD

Humans want to serve cats; it is the natural order of things. Unfortunately many people do not have a furry one to care for and consequently find that their lives lack meaning, purpose and direction.

If this is your current situation I urge you not to panic. There are many ways in which one might acquire a kitty to care for, including rescue shelters (where lost cats and abandoned kittens are available for adoption), as well as pet shops and breeders; and of course some people just open their door and welcome in the stray that stays.

If acquiring a kitty of your own is not possible you may be able to give service to a friend's cat now and again, volunteer at a shelter, or even book an hour at one of the new, much touted cat petting cafes. The epidemic of humans suffering from severe cat deficiency has reached such a point that cat petting cafes are now cropping up all over the world. You can now book an hour of kitty time anywhere from Australia Austria, China, France, Germany, Japan, Russia, Taiwan, Thailand, and the UK, to the USA and beyond!

Whatever your situation is there are certain issues to be considered when acquiring a new kitty. Whether it's making sure your new cat is healthy, or simply knowing how to introduce a new cat to the currently reigning monarch of your household, these things need to be done properly.

Only after you have given the prospect of cat ownership thorough consideration and have decided that you have the time, the money, the stability of circumstance and the emotional resources to undertake such a responsibility should you even consider shopping for a cat.

Rather than choosing a new cat you should probably let the cat do the choosing. If your chosen one doesn't warm to you for some reason he will probably just leave you and move in with your neighbors, so letting the cat do the choosing is a sensible approach.

When meeting your potential kitty for the first time, offer him the back of your hand to sniff (at a distance of at least 2-3 inches) and see how he responds. If he steps forward, takes a sniff and starts head butting you, you are probably at the beginning of a beautiful friendship. On the other hand if he hisses or recoils then he is probably not meant to be your cat.

Shelters and rescue centres

If you are out to acquire a new kitty this is by far my preferred option. There are a world of lost cats and abandoned kittens that need loving homes. Most rescue centers will make sure all cats they adopt out are fully health checked, wormed, de-sexed and micro chipped before they are sent out; which is especially important if you already have another cat at home. The last thing you want to do is expose your current cat to new diseases.

By choosing a rescue cat you are also helping to stamp out unscrupulous kitty farms with cruel breeding practices. At least if you get your kitty from the shelter you will know you are not putting your money behind such barbarity.

Pet Shops

Pet shops often have super cute little kittens in the window, but I urge you to resist the impulse purchase. In taking on a kitten you are entering a life of indentured service, and much like becoming a priest or a nun this really shouldn't be done on a whim.

I am not generally a fan of acquiring kittens through pet shops. Depending on where you live pet shops may or not be regulated with regard to animal welfare. It is worth finding this out as many unregulated pet shops source cats from unscrupulous breeders whose practices can be quite cruel. Over breeding mother cats and removing kittens far too young, (which can lead to behavioral and health problems in adult life), are common issues. Be on the alert for kittens that are very tiny or still have blue eyes, as they are probably still a bit young to be away from their mothers.

You should always ask the pet shop where they source their animals and get them to provide documentary evidence that their kittens have been de-sexed, and had their initial round of vaccinations.

Breeders

Purebred show cats with papers can be mind bogglingly expensive to buy, and some breeds are prone to certain health issues, so you may need very deep pockets to go down this route.

If you have your heart set on a certain breed of cat you will most probably have to go through a breeder. However some avaricious breeders treat their pure breed cats with utter disregard, keeping them constantly locked up and pregnant with no quality of life, and as soon as they are too old to breed they are unceremoniously destroyed. This practice is akin to factory farming, and it is cruel and inhumane. It offers the poor fluffy one no quality of life whatsoever.

While there are caring reputable breeders out there you will need to be careful, as many will simply tell you what you want to hear. Check for yourself, do the research; after all the last thing you want is your hard earned money going to support cruelty to kitties!

If you can do without the look of a breed, a moggy will often have fewer health problems, be less likely to be stolen (this can be a problem with breeds, my sister has lost three silver point Burmese over the years), and of course moggies are just as beautiful and will love you just as much.

However if you simply must have a purebred Bengal, then make sure that it comes from a reputable, cruelty free breeder, has had enough time with its mother, has had all its shots, and has been wormed, micro chipped and de-sexed, (if you don't intend to have it breed that is) before you collect him.

Lost and Found

It is quite a big deal for a cat to condescend to accepting your service and if you do not perform to their satisfaction you may find that your cat will enlist the services of other humans. Your cat may even up stumps and move house. We are currently in the service of two such cats who rejected their initial staff in favor of our humble service.

If a cat chooses to sack its staff and engage your services, it is essential that you let the former staff know that their fluffy overload is in fact safe and cared for. The poor dears are probably in a panic-stricken frenzy, unable to sleep or eat with torment over their kitty's inexplicable absence.

There is of course also the chance your new foundling may not have willingly left its former home; he may simply have got lost and is unable to find his way back. If this is the case your new fluffy friend may be overjoyed to see his former staff arriving at your door. He may also feel a little overwhelmed and guilty and he may even hide.

But just because a cat hides when he sees his old carers doesn't necessarily mean he doesn't like them, he could just find the whole situation a bit overwhelming.

Most of the time a cat's former carer can be tracked down through its microchip (if it has one). Most vets have a chip reader and will scan the furry one for free. Once you have found your new cat's previous carer you can let them know their cat is safe, and negotiate his majesty's future living arrangements from there.

INTRODUCING A NEW KITTY TO THE ROYAL HOUSEHOLD

If you are already blessed with fluffy ones but you feel you could accommodate even more cat action in your world, you should not assume your existing felines feel the same way.

Any new addition to the royal household will most likely be met with suspicion, hissing and great deal of annoyance. You are their human, and now you want to go off moonlighting with some other cat? This is brazen disloyalty in the eyes of your cat, and will not be taken lightly. I have even known much-loved cats to leave home upon the arrival of a new kitten in the household.

There are however a few tricks to smoothing out the process of transition, and making the whole ordeal less traumatic for Mr Fluffy Pants.

When you first bring home the new arrival, keep him separated from any incumbent royal kitties. It is best if you can keep your new kitty confined to just one room. Put your new kitty's feeding bowl near the door and move your reigning royal's feeding station to the other side of the door. If there is a special treat food that you can place in your reigning kitty's bowl when you finally let him go and sniff the door, he will come to associate the smell of the new cat with food and treats. This will help a lot when it comes time to introduce them.

Keep feeding the cats on opposite sides of the door for at least a day or two, until they are both quite comfortable with the arrangement. Then slowly open the door a crack at feeding time to allow them to safely sniff each other. There may be a bit of hissing to begin with, but it usually won't last too long. Don't let them stay together too long at this point, maybe only for five to ten minutes. Over the next few days gradually increase the opening of the door until they are both eating at an open door, in plain sight of each other, and allow them to interact for increasing levels of time in larger areas of the house after food.

Through this gradual process of allowing the new cat to slowly enter the territory, you can avoid a lot of unnecessary trauma to your existing kitty, and give your new kitty a safe space in which to feel at home while he gets accustomed to his new servants and surroundings. This whole process should take somewhere between one and two weeks.

During that time it is important not to just lock your new cat in an empty room. If you have a room like an office that you use during the day, the new cat can get to know you, and feel comfortable with you before it has to deal with integrating into the household cat hierarchy. If you are putting the new cat in the spare room, make sure you go in and spend time with her.

Taking your time to introduce a new cat into the household won't guarantee they will get along, but it will go a long way to easing what can be a very traumatic situation for both cats.

THE CAT FRIENDLY HOUSE

Whether you have an indoor or outdoor cat you need to make the home comfortable and accommodating for his royal fluffiness. A suitable house will require safe time out zones, where your kitty can hide from the dog, the visitors, the kids, the other cats and even you.

There will need places to sit that are high up. This is not just because they wish to look down on you, (although make no mistake, they do want to look down on you), it is because before domestication cats used to climb trees to rest safely away from predators. "High sitting" is encoded into their DNA, and some cats will get quite agitated if they cannot find some high perch on which to reside.

As far as furnishings go it is better to provide things for your kitty to scratch than to chastise them for clawing things. There are some very effective ways to discourage the fluff ball clawing your silk sofa, but we will get into that later.

Lastly if your cat is kept in full time or even just overnight she will need somewhere private, a good distance from her feeding station, for a litter box.

As you can see the basic requirements of a cat friendly house are not arduous, meaning that most modestly placed humans are more than able to comfortably accommodate a feline. Meow!

Loud Noises

As a carer it is your duty to maintain a peaceful and harmonious environment. For the most part this means no loud or sudden unexplained banging, no circular saws, no angle grinders, no nail guns, no guns in general, no blenders, no popcorn makers, no sounds of unknown dogs approaching, and no unexpected noises from the cat door. All of these things can be deeply disturbing to a kitty.

However the sound of the microwave whirring for 10 seconds, while taking the chill off their fresh meat is acceptable.

The Vacuum

Your vacuum is unquestionably the pinnacle of evil. It is the son of Satan, the most hateful thing ever to grace the face of the planet. Its violent roar is the ultimate torture, a punishment so vile and unbearable that leaping into the arms of death would come as a welcome relief.

Of course the fact that you seem quite ok with the sound of Armageddon fast approaching is totally unfathomable to your kitty. Why would you even have such a heinous implement in the house?

There are however some among the feline brethren that have turned to the dark side. These godless creatures not only tolerate the evil one, they actively seek it out, either hopping on top of it like it is some kind of carnival ride, or pressing their servers to indulge them in unholy acts of ritual cleansing.

The fact is, if your cat allows its fur to be vacuumed he has clearly strayed from the righteous path, either that or he has gone completely mad. While an exorcism is probably not warranted, keeping him away from the vacuum should go some way to curbing any incipient evil, and it should stop the neighbors gossiping.

Scritching and a scratching

Kitties are renowned for destroying furniture with their incessant clawing. This is not due an unbridled contempt for your hard earned furnishing dollar; it is simply natural for cats to scratch. It helps keep their claws in good order and it provides a good upper body stretch and work out.

Some people think that Ms Fluff's refusal to use the cat scratching post is some form of feline malevolence but this is rarely the case. Mostly there is something about the scratching post they do not like. The most common issue is that the base of their scratching post is not big enough and doesn't have enough weight in it to provide adequate resistance

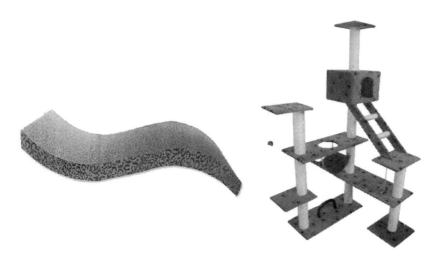

unlike your sofa which will not move no matter how hard kitty claws it. Sometimes it is the material of the post they may not like. Some cats like rope or sisal, some cats love timer or fabric, so it can take a bit of trial and error to find the perfect scratcher for his royal highness.

If you are desperate to keep the claws off the sofa one of the best ways is put "sticky paws" on the couch in the area the cat is attracted to. "Sticky paws" is a double sided tape made especially for deterring cats and their claws. It won't leave sticky goop on your furniture, but the cats don't like the feel of it and will quickly move on. For this strategy to really work it is best if you can put one or two scratching posts right next to where you are trying to stop them scratching.

Another thing to consider is that some cats like their scratching stations to be vertical while others like them horizontal. Our cat Mauser is a vertical girl and has an old fence paling in the garden, Podge on the other hand is strictly a horizontal man, and the only way we could stop him clawing the carpet was to give him the kick board from my swimming kit. If you have the room it can be good to combine a scratching post, a hiding place and somewhere high to sit in a single cat tower.

Visitors

To cats, visitors are either terrifying unwelcome interlopers, or an opportunity to garner further praise and expand their circle of ardent admirers. If your cats love visitors you must banish everyone with cat allergies from your home, as kitty would be most upset to be shut out of the action.

However if your kitty doesn't like visitors make sure she has somewhere safe to hide. And most importantly keep visiting children well away.

GROOMING

Cats are very particular about grooming. For most cats the practice of self grooming takes up about 50% of their waking hours. However this does not let you off the hook.

Brushing you cat

Your cats will need extra attention from you, in the form of incessant brushing, the occasional bath, the cleaning and maintaining of any clothing or collars and the clipping of claws and fur (should it be necessary).

Brushing your kitty is a serious responsibility. Failing to brush your cat regularly can lead to hairballs. This is not just unpleasant for your furry one; you will suffer too. After all no-one likes cleaning lakes of regurgitated bile and fur off their lovely shag pile carpet!

While most cats love being brushed and will run up enthusiastically the moment the brush comes out of the drawer, others are more

cautious about the process. There could be a number of reason your cat resists being brushed. It could be that they have some sore spots or scratches under their fur, it could be that the brush pulls on their fur, or it could be that you are simply using the wrong brush or brushing in the wrong way.

There are many different types of brush you can use on your kitty and most cats will have a personal favorite. The very fine toothcombs are excellent for removing excess hair, fleas and their eggs; but you will need to brush firmly to remove them and many cats will resist. The brushes with the short steel bristles are very good for hair removal, but once again you will need to brush reasonably firmly.

If you are meeting resistance then I recommend starting with a steel loop brush (also known as a shedding blade). While brushing gently with a steel loop is quite acceptable to most cats, it will still remove large amounts of loose fur.

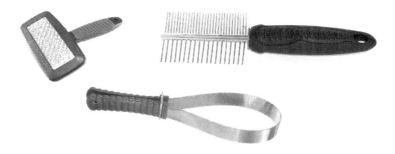

Initially some cats find whole body brushing over stimulating. The long body strokes can really set their nerves on edge. If your cat is particularly sensitive to brushing try slowly introducing your cat to the idea by concentrating on small areas around the top of the head and the back of the neck (and possibly even under the chin). As the head and neck are the main areas your cat enjoys being petted on, focusing on these areas will help your cat will come to see brushing as a treat.

Once your cat is totally used to the head and neck brushing you can start to slowly introduce the occasional full-length body stroke. If you start out slowly and gently there is every chance that over time your cat will come to love being brushed

Bathing your cat.

Washing a cat is not a fun undertaking and should be avoided unless absolutely necessary. Occasionally cats will get something noxious on their fur, or get ringworm or some other infection that requires an antifungal bath, but proceed with caution. Never use human shampoo, as it is often not suitable for felines due to strong perfumes and differences in the pH. Instead use a mild non-scented pet soap, or a pure castile soap, taking care to avoid the eyes. After you have kitty lathered up rinse her off thoroughly with warm water, once again taking care to avoid her eyes and ears. Once she is rinsed and has shaken the excess water off she will usually enjoy being rubbed down with a towel. To help you avoid her ire you may want to give her a treat afterwards.

You should know that your cat will HATE being bathed, and retribution will likely be both demonstrable and swift. You will most likely be met with claws, and may even discover some random deposit of cat faeces in your favourite shoes afterwards; but it's a small price to pay to make sure your kitty is OK.

When bathing a cat there are a few precautions you should take to minimize the risk of getting seriously clawed. Firstly make sure you are protected. In trying to escape the bath there is every chance your cat may attempt to claw it's way up your arms to escape over your shoulders. A thick fleece, rubber gloves, and a towel around your shoulders, will give any claws something other than your skin to sink into. And keep the water moderate in temperature, not too hot not too cold. Using a small trough or large bucket (rather than the bath) will help keep water spills and splashes to a minimum, and standing on a non slip rubber mat will help avoid your slipping over.

The kitty mani –pedi

Cats use their claws for just about everything they do, from scratching that itch, to climbing a fence, so declawing can be quite traumatic for a cat. There has been a lot of debate about declawing cats but I am not personally in favor of it.

Some people labor under the impression that declawing is a simple matter of removing a cat's nails, kind of like having your fingernails trimmed. Unfortunately this is not the case. Declawing a cat is usually done by amputating the last bone of each toe; which is kind of like having your fingers chopped off to the knuckle. It is a cruel and unnecessary surgery that provides no medical benefit to the cat and in many countries the practice has been banned. Declawing may also have unwanted side effects, such as making your cat less likely to use its litter box.

However if little Miss Scratchy's inability to keep her claws off the couch is driving you nuts, there are other options. Educated kitty carers can easily train their cats to use their claws in a manner that allows everyone in the household to live together happily.

(for other sofa saving strategies go to "scratching and scritching" in the chapter on playing).

Clipping kitty's claws is one far less cruel option. It is much more like fingernail trimming than full declawing. By holding kitty's feet between your thumb and forefinger and pressing gently you should be able get her claws to come out. You can then gently snip their ends, taking special care not to cut them too short or into the white at the centre of her claws, which can cause kitty's claws to bleed. You can use a specially designed cat claw clipper or just a regular large nail clipper. Either way it is best to take this procedure slowly, only doing one or two claws in each sitting. If you feel uncertain about doing it yourself most vets or groomers can show you how to do it properly, or you can simply get them to do it for you. For kittens you should not use clippers, instead just give their claws a gentle file.

It can take some time for cats to get used to having their feet handled, as it is not something they usually like. The best way to train them into it is to gently give their feet a quick squeeze when they are being petted and are very relaxed. It's better if you don't try to clip their claws every time you touch their feet, so if you give them a small treat after they let you squeeze their feet they will come to associate foot play with treats and the whole thing will get a lot easier.

Claw caps are another option. These soft gel caps are fitted over a cat's claws to stop them gripping onto things (and therefore tearing up the furniture). They last about 2 months before they fall off and will need to be replaced. While claw caps won't hurt your cat they will prevent him from grabbing things; and as cats exercise their upper bodies by pulling against whatever they can dig their claws into, claw caps may interfere with your cat's upper body muscle tone.

PETTING

To the uninitiated petting a cat may look like a simple enough affair, but no. Cat petting is an art-form that takes years of practice to master. While your cat may occasionally tolerate your ham-fisted attempts, there is no doubt he would prefer it if you took a class or two before letting yourself loose on his royal personage.

There are so many variables one needs to master. The speed, the pressure, the placement; all of these are crucial to successful petting. And of course your technique will need to be specifically tuned and adjusted to each individual cat.

Many novices fail to recognise the delicate, detailed nuances of cat petting and thus end up with a quick nip or a swipe of claws. A hapless neophyte may assume that the cat is simply displaying its mercurial nature, however the rules of cat care clearly state that even if a kitty appears to have randomly attacked you, it is never their fault. You obviously did something wrong!

When to pet

Much the same as it is with the Queen of England; the first rule of cat petting is that you never touch first. You should always try and wait for Her Majesty to initiate contact.

A sure sign your cat is up for some attention is when she gives you a good head butting. Admittedly this is not a subtle signal, but it is not meant to be. Kitty wants attention, NOW! What ever you are doing is simply not important! You should stop it immediately and make with the snuggles. However if that is not possible you should at a bare minimum give kitty a few quick strokes just to let her know you are not ignoring her.

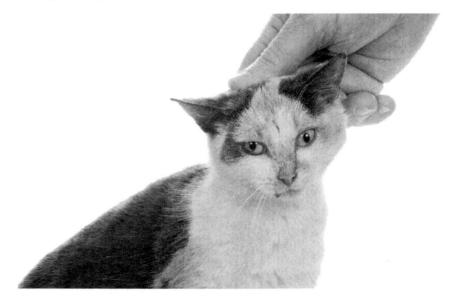

But beware, not all contact is an invitation. Just because Flufferella jumps up onto your lap and lies down, this does not necessarily mean she wants you to start petting her. It could be that you are merely a wonderful heated seat on which she wants to lie down and relax. If she starts to twitch, fidget or flick her tail when you stroke her, STOP IMMEDIATELY! Just let her sit on you quietly, and be grateful.

Remember any contact is strictly on Her Majesty's terms. You must always seek permission to touch her and know that she is always in control of the interaction.

You can however encourage your cat to accept more of your affection by offering her the back of your hand to sniff. If she either ignores your offering, hisses at you, or recoils from your hand with a suspicious glare a wise servant would reconsider petting her at this time.

However, if she meows, sniffs your hand and then rubs her chin or head against it, or perhaps brushes the side of her body up against you, the chances are she is open to a little affection.

If you get the green light you may then, and only then, open the palm of your hand and gently touch her. Start with the chin, head and neck area and if you get a positive response you can then move on to a few whole body strokes.

I like it like that!

There are a few places that cats just love being touched. Conveniently most of these places just happen to be where they have scent glands; a fact your cat will exploit mercilessly in marking you out as their property. Know that when you pet your cat in the following places you are in fact being branded, cat style.

The Chin:

Oh how kitty loves a chin scritching! Cats will often rub their jaws onto your hand, (in case you are too stupid to figure out that is what they want). They can tolerate hours of gently rubbing in the chin and jaw area, so have a good breakfast and be prepared for a long shift.

The top of the head:

With their markedly superior intelligence and all that deep philosophical musing, sometimes cats need a bit of a rub down to relieve the pressure on their overworked grey matter. A light scritching between and behind the ears will be a soothing treat for your fluffy one.

Pay particular focus to the base of the ears, as there are some really good scent glands there. If you miss the spot your cat may head butt you to get you properly marked.

The cheek of it:

A bit of cheek scritching can set your cats whiskers twirling with delight. In cat world, the practice of running the back of your hand across her cheeks is totally sublime. It's a surefire way to get a rumbling purr from an otherwise reserved feline.

A tail of two kitties:

Depending on the cat, applying a bit of a scritch to the base of their tail is either a divine heavenly treat or an unbearable torture. If your kitty is one of the ones who loves it you will be rewarded with a purr so loud it will wake the neighbors. However if your kitty is in the other camp you can expect a quick nip or biff as your cat bids a hasty retreat.

When venturing beyond the head and neck areas certain positions and petting styles are distinctly more pleasing to some cats than others.

Taking sides: Lying on ones side is a clear indication that carers may attempt petting. But please, light strokes and only on the up facing side of your cat!

From forehead to tail: After briefly petting the forehead you may attempt to run your hand along the spine down to the base of the tail. You can try gently scritching as you bring your hand down along the cat's back, but keep it moving, don't stop on your way down.

You can also try massaging her neck muscles by pinching gently as you move down the back. If your cat likes it she may even arch his back to add a bit more pressure to your hand.

However if he pulls his ears back, flicks his tail or cowers away from your hand, I am afraid you have not pleased his lordship. You should immediately stop what you are doing, put on a hair shirt and proceed to flog yourself mercilessly as punishment for your failure.

Don't touch me there!

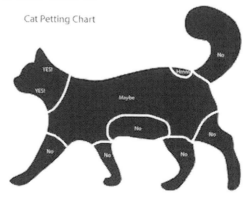

Cat Petting Chart

Just as we may wince at the idea of being touched on certain parts of our bodies, our kitties are the same. While there is some variation from cat to cat on what is acceptable touching, there are some no go zones that are fairly universal.

As a general rule you should try to avoid the tail, the feet and the belly.

Tall tails:

While many cats love a bit of a scritch at the base of the tail, some do not. If you are game enough to try tail petting be prepared for a festival of low pitched growling, teeth and claws. To state the manifestly obvious, if Mr Fuffypants flinches, hisses or meows angrily, or if his tail starts to thump up and down or swish from side to side, then STOP IT IMMEDIATELY! Avoid touching him there in future, and warn your guests that his tail is a no-go zone!

Belly up:

When a cat is super relaxed and feeling safe it might roll onto its back and give you a nice view of its belly. When your cat does this it is important to remember that your cat is not a dog. Dogs love a belly scritching. Cats? Eh, not so much!

With all the vital organs located in the cat's stomach region it is quite a vulnerable area. It is a cat's natural instinct to protect its belly from predators and a lot of cats will instinctively make with the teeth and claws if you touch them there.

There is the occasional eccentric oddball cat that does like a bit of belly rub, but be warned they will most likely interpret it as an invitation to play rough. In the spirit of a good healthy wrestling match there is every chance you will be greeted with a vigorous round of teeth and claws. This may not be an attack; it may simply be your cat's way of rough housing with you.

If a cat hooks onto you with its claws, hold still and let the cat disengage herself. If she does not withdraw her claws you may need to reach over and gently pull the paw back to unhook her. Cats can often scratch deeply, even when they were not intending to, particularly when they get overstimulated. When the claws come out the best policy is always to stop moving.

Tread carefully

Approach your cat's feet with caution. Many cats don't like their feet touched at all. You should never play with a cat's feet unless you know the cat, and are reasonably sure she likes it.

Most cats can be slowly trained into having their feet handled for activities like claw clipping. The trick is to introduce the idea over a few weeks or months (depending on the temperament and amenability of your cat), while offering small tasty rewards for their compliance.

Start by petting your kitty to get him relaxed, then seek permission to stroke his feet by touching one of his feet with your finger. If the cat doesn't object you can lightly pet that foot in a downward direction.

If he pulls his foot away, flattens his ears, hisses or walks away it is time to stop and try again later.

Signs Mr Fluffy does not want to be petted any more:

Something that is often misunderstood by kitty care givers is that more attention is not necessarily better. While your cat may love being petted there are times when it all gets to be a bit much. Cats are very prone to overstimulation, so what can feel good one moment can become highly irritating the next. This is particularly true of the full body sweep.

If you see your cat issuing any of the following warnings, take heed! Otherwise you are likely to come in for a sharp biting or a swipe of claws.

Ears pulled down or flat to the head

Tail swishing, flicking or twitching

Fidgeting or extending claws

Growling or hissing (not that I really needed to tell you that one)

Petting Tips:

Petting the cat is a symbiotic affair. While clearly the benefits to the cat are foremost in a good servant's mind, the fact is that petting your pet can release endorphins, lower your blood pressure, and reduce the likelihood of a heart attack or stroke.

While some cats just love to be picked up, others clearly do not. If a cat attempts to jump out of your arms, or wriggle away this is a clear sign that he doesn't want to be held by you at this time, so put kitty down! Any low-pitched meowing could indicate your cat is angry, but then again maybe not. Understanding certain signals from your cat can be as confusing as learning english as a second language. While some cats will meow when they want you to pet harder, others meow when they want you to stop. If you are in any doubt it is probably better to stop, just in case.

When petting your cat pay attention to any unusual reactions or newly sensitive areas. If your cat complains or withdraws or even bites or scratches your cat may have a fresh wound or injury (particularly if it is an outside cat). If you have any concerns or find any abscesses it is best to take your cat to the vet for a check up.

If you want to pet a cat that you do not know well, you may need to be patient. Most cats will tolerate a good deal more petting from their servants than they do from a visitor.

CAT'S PLAY

As far as your cat is concerned playing is a serious job. It is the kitty equivalent of work. It enhances a cat's mental agility, keeps their hunting skills sharpened and most importantly it staves off the inherent tedium of being so markedly superior.

There are a number of popular cat games that we humans often fail to see the point of; but just because our brains don't have the sophistication to fully appreciate the finer points of "cat in a bag", doesn't mean it is not a totally engrossing pastime for our feline friends.

Cat in a bag

It is a truth universally understood that a cat in need of place to sit would prefer to sit in a bag! After all bags feel safe, warm and secure and who wouldn't want that? But what is it exactly about bag sitting that is so irresistible to cats?

The old saying "the cat's in the bag" means that an important confidence is being safely kept, or that some desired outcome has either been achieved or is now imminent.

On the other hand the expression "letting the cat out of the bag", is generally not considered to be such a good thing, and is usually only used when someone has revealed an unwelcome or unpalatable truth.

So what can we infer from these two these two well-worn allegorical quips? It's quite simple really:

A cat IN the bag = good.

A cat OUT of the bag = bad!

This, my friends, is one of the most profound truths ever gleaned by the likes of man; and while humanity may have wrestled throughout the ages to expand this truth into a workable set of metaphors, your cat understands it innately. Cat in a bag is totally awesome!

That said not all bags are created equal. Recyclable shopping bags are totally fabulous, little mesh Oroton bags, not so much. Large paper or plastic bags are great, tiny draw-string jewelry bags are utterly useless.

Cat in a box

A popular variation of cat in a bag is cat in a box!

Cat in a box has actually been around since boxes where first invented. There are some who claim boxes where originally invented just for cats to sit in and it wasn't until several hundred years later that some bright spark realized they could be put to other uses.

Over the years the practice of feline box sitting has taken on an almost religious dimension. The mere sight of an empty box is enough to have Mr Fluffypants scuttling to pay homage to this ancient and hallowed ritual; it is practically encoded into feline DNA!

Such is the fluffy one's fever for the activity you can even see the tiniest of kittens eagerly clamoring to embrace the practice. They need no instruction or encouragement from their elders; they just inherently KNOW box sitting is a good thing to do!

Being meticulously clean creatures, any cardboard boxes should be changed regularly for your cat's optimum box sitting pleasure. On average a cardboard box will last about a week before it will need to be replaced.

Kill O'clock

Like most royal lineages, felines have some quirky genetic predispositions that have been with them throughout the ages. One such peculiarity is the rather eccentric observance of "Kill O'Clock".

Kill O'Clock is a specific time of day when a ritual madness descends over all the felines within the confines of the royal household. It is characterized by a thundering stampede of paws, as any cat present repeatedly barrels from one end of the house to the other. This curious habit is largely an exercise in feline efficiency. As cats tend to spend a minimum of 16 hours a day napping, and goodly proportion of the remaining hours engaged in self-grooming, Kill O'Clock is an excellent way to cram a full days aerobic exertion into less than ten minutes.

While most of the time it is a harmless burn off of excess energy, there can be play fighting, hissing, biffing, growling, claws and in extreme cases real fighting between the cats engaged in this ritual, but it is rarely serious.

However Kill O'Clock does require some level of human oversight. It can traverse many levels, from the floor to the table to the top of the crystal cabinet, any loose or unanchored objects will be unceremoniously thrown from their place. Its aftermath can be similar to that of a small tornado.

Usually occurring shortly before or after meal times the apparent demonic possession of your fluffy one never lasts too long. It can in fact be quite entertaining to watch.

Cat and Mouse

As humans we don't usually warm to having mice in the house. We tend to think of them as filthy, cable gnawing pests that poo everywhere. But is that mouse really an unwanted disease-spreading rodent, or is it actually a fresh tasty treat that doubles as a play-thing?

The answer depends largely on who you ask. Like most cats, if you ask our Mauser and Podge they will tell you no house is complete without the odd mouse roaming about. Having mice in the house is practically essential for keeping a cat entertained when it's too cold to go out.

So strongly do Mauser and Podge believe this, if they happen to find there are no mice inside they will actually go outside and bring one in.

For Mauser and Podge the acquisition of a new mouse is a festive celebration. They gather round it singing loudly, making sure we know all about their extraordinary hunting prowess. After we provide them with effusive torrents of admiration for their stunning achievement, they usually let the mouse go!

If they ultimately fail to recapture and eat the poor thing, the mouse eventually scuttles underneath the nearest piece of furniture and promptly dies. While an inaccessible dead mouse rarely pleases humans, (mostly due to the delightful aroma and the visceral stains on the carpet), this turn of events is a stunning victory in cat world. If the mouse actually dies inside without you noticing, a week later your cat gets to hunt countless flies; and those kitties loves hunting flies!

A hunting we will go!

Our cat Podge is a consummate hunter. He can stalk a wall for hours on end. With a laser like focus he stares, crouched and ready for the moment when that wall makes its move. So far the wall has yet to do anything untoward, but rest assured, when it does Podge will be ready for it!

While most cats will hunt pretty well anything, not all cats are wall stalkers. Some require movement to activate their hunting drive, feathers on the end of a string, a fly, your ankles, even the dog. You name it, if it moves they will stalk it, and duly pounce.

If your home doesn't have a lot of things for your fluffy one to hunt, it is your duty to provide a viable range of huntable options. This could include any number of animated or wind up cat toys, non threatening canines, another cat, a feather on a string, a fish in a bowl, an infestation of oversized cockroaches or a small mouse plague.

If however you are struggling to find a suitable option, the hand under the duvet/blanket hunt can be implemented without any additional outlay. When your kitty is near simply place your hand under the duvet or a blanket and move it slightly. Keep moving it every few seconds until your cat fixates on the movement. After a short time your cat will likely pounce on your hand in a gleeful leap of teeth and claws. As you cat may not realize it is your hand under there, I recommend a thick Duvet or thick gloves for this one.

Hide and don't seek

Whether it is the pressure of royal duties, or just the fact that the dog is an annoying idiot, every cat needs to get away from it all once in a while. Cats just love to get into secret nooks where they can curl up secure in the knowledge that neither you, nor that imbecilic K9 will bother them.

Like all great artists and philosophers, cats love their private time. It gives them a chance to mull thinks over, study up on their interests, and plot new ways to test the limits of your pandering.

A cat that is hiding does not want to be disturbed, and as a dutiful servant you must make sure all junior servants (AKA children) understand this. A cat that is hiding may feel quite scared and skittish. It is much better to coax kitty out that to drag her out. A cat should never be forcibly pulled out of its hiding place unless absolutely necessary for their health and safety.

The red dot

Most cats go nuts for a laser torch. Chasing the red dot is almost as good as a paint ball session is to a 15 year old boy who is overdosing on testosterone. If however your cat is aggressively intelligent he will pretty soon figure out he is effectively jumping at shadows and quickly lose interest, but if your cat is not a candidate for the Mensa test then it's pure endless joy and fun. Your average feline will leap, run, stalk, jump and enjoy a damn good work out.

Walking the cat

Contrary to popular opinion there are cats that love going for walks. Many indoor cat owners like to take their cats outside on the leash for the occasional walk, although my husband has trained all our outdoor cats into walking with him without a leash. They will actually follow him over ½ a mile from our house. (This practice is really for suburban or country cats only, not for downtown inner city cats).

If you move slowly enough for your cat to explore as you go, and take a route that provides lots of cover most cats can be encouraged to walk around the block off leash. Start out by just walking slowly a few houses down as your cats follow. Everyday extend the range a little further and soon enough you will be taking your cats all the way around the block.

In our neighborhood the sight of my husband out walking a small army of cats causes about as much amusement as it does utter amazement. Their route is peppered with other cats and dogs. Some of the local felines regularly come out to say hello to the passing parade; and some desperately want to tag along. As for the dogs, well let's just say they know their place!

SLEEPING

While it is a cat's prerogative to sleep wherever and whenever they please, the same privilege is not extended to you, (particularly if you have been assigned the breakfast shift).

In case you hadn't noticed cats don't do insomnia. In fact they can spend up to 18 hours a day sleeping, so they are kind of snoozing experts. When so much of their time is dedicated to gentle slumber it is easy to understand why cats need a minimum of ten different places dotted through the house in which to grab a quick nap.

Not only must you provide an endless array of sleeping options, they must be kept impeccably clean.

Cats have many preferred sleeping places, but not many of them would be where you might choose. While you may labor under the delusion that you own some of your cat's beds, understand that this is not true. As far as your cat is concerned you exist at their pleasure and all that is yours is theirs. To give a few examples.

Your bed is mine

Yes your cat will sleep on your pillow, on your head, on your chest, between you and your partner, under the duvet, over the duvet, in fact your cat will sleep anywhere it damn well pleases!

What we humans often don't recognize is that cats like to play a game called "human pretzel". This is where their humans go to bed comfortably, and over the course of the night the cat will slowly maneuver itself into positions that force you to move ever so slightly.

The cat will repeat this several times over the course of the night until you are tied up like a pretzel in a corner of the bed. Meanwhile her majesty is splayed out across the sheets like a snow angel. The message is clear, "the bed is mine".

Your sofa is mine

If you think for one moment you have some kind of claim on your couch think again. No, really... Think about it! If you really had dominion over "your" sofa would its side look like a scrap of shag pile carpet?

Exactly! The fact that an oversized scratching post has alternate uses, such as providing comfortable seating for humans, is merely a convenient coincidence. Your cat knows there is simply no better implement for sharpening claws than a couch, and the newer and more expensive the better.

Your lap is mine

A cat is a lap's raison d'être, for without a cat a lap would have no purpose whatsoever. Should a cat ever deign to utilize your lap you are one the fortunate souls whose life has been imbued with a meaning and purpose beyond the mundane. You are a cat couch! Con-cat-ulations!

When you are in the service of a cat, you need to understand that your lap is not your own. It must be ready at all times to provide a heated throne for His Majesty. If for some reason your lap is not immediately available, understand that your laptop will be enlisted into service instead. While it is not the same as your lap, it is warm and it smells of you, and will therefore do until you can make yourself available.

Your chest is mine

"I will sleep on your chest when ever it pleases me! To be clear, when I say your chest, what I mean is all your chests! Not just the one that houses your lungs, but any treasure chest, blanket box, armoire, chest of draws etc. The lot, they are all mine, yes all of them, along with all that is contained within said chests."

Make no mistake, this is your cat's position on this and any resistance on your part will be met with shameless displays of your cat's manifest right to everything you think you possess.

Your fresh laundry is mine!

Fresh baskets of laundry exist for the sole purpose of providing your cat another place to sleep. You may wear your clothes once your cat has finished infusing them with her own delicate aroma, but not before.

There are good and practical reasons for this. When you venture out the front door (to go on one of those totally inexplicable visits to the vet), there is every chance you may come across another cat.

Just as people use wedding rings to symbolize that they are not available for marriage, cats use their scent to let other cats know you are not available to serve them. Thus all laundry should remain in the basket for a period of no more or less than 2 days, which is sufficient time for your cat to place their stamp on it.

More than two to three days, and well really, that is just gross! Cats are not hippies! You cannot possibly expect them to sit somewhere for more than three days without providing a layer of clean linen.

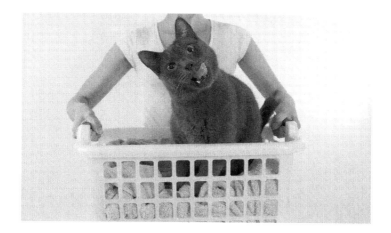

TALKING CAT

The Purr

When your cat starts to rumble she is telling you something. Traditionally we understand a good hearty purr to be a sign of great pleasure, but purring can also be a sign of extreme stress. As a cat carer it is your job to know which kind of purr your puss is emanating at any given moment.

If you are in any doubt whether you are about to be killed or cuddled you should look for other clearer forms of cat communication. If your furry one exhibits a flicking or thumping tail, flattened ears and drawn claws you should probably start drawing up your will. On the other hand if she rolls over and shows you her belly, head butts you, does the ankle weave or starts to practice extreme frottage on your leg then you may be in for an extended kitty snuggle fest. Although don't assume, sometimes kitty just wants a quick greeting.

As a general rule the louder the rumble, the happier the cat. A soft purr means that your fluff ball is content and you are relatively safe. A loud purr means your furry one is quite happy, thank you very much. However an sonic boom of a purr could mean kitty is getting way over excited, which can easily flip over into irritation and annoyance, so be careful, those kitty teeth and claws can emerge in a nanosecond.

The cat's meow

A cat's meow is a special gift. They do not meow at each other, or at any other animal, only at humans. It is their "human" voice if you like.

While cats remain largely frustrated that we have yet to develop a sufficient level of telepathy to understand their every waking whim and desire, they have worked out that they can snap us to attention with a well pitched meow! Our cat Mauser has this down to a fine art. Like a baby's cry we understand the intonation in each and every utterance. The "feed me NOW" meow is totally different to the "pick me up" meow.

The flicky tail

There are many levels and gradations of the flicky tail, but fundamentally they all come down to this is a very clear message, "STOP what ever you are doing, and BACK OFF ... or face the consequences"

Kneading -The language of kitty love

Kitties love to knead on things when they feel happy, comfortable and secure. Blankets, bellies, legs, beds, duvets, dressing gowns. You name it, if kitty likes it she will pad on it from time to time.

The reason for this behavior is not actually known, but the most popular theory is that cats associate kneading with the comfort and security of suckling their mother as kittens. While it's clearly something kitty does when she is happy, unfortunately for your belly the happier she is the more the claws come out. But then again, we all know love hurts!

TRAVEL AND YOUR CAT

The first thing you must understand is that while the job of cat carer may not pay, it is for life. Brief holidays are permitted, but if you go away for more than a day or two your cat will think that you have gone stark raving mad. Your cat is fully aware that lavishing them with endless doting care is your life's primary purpose; so other than going completely bonkers what reason could you possibly have for abandoning your post?

If you absolutely must travel, know that your cat would much prefer to stay at home, and it is your job to enlist the services of a feeder to undertake your duties while you are away. If other arrangements cannot be made, and you have no choice but to send Princess Kitty to a "cat hotel" know that you will probably be punished upon your return.

Once your kitty is happily settled back in at home and has gotten over the initial joy of seeing you again, the retribution will begin in earnest. Depending on your cat's temperament and the length of your absence, your punishment could be anything from a short period of mild snubbing right though to an all out terrorist attack, resulting in hairballs, urine and other bodily excreta winding up in places you really don't want them.

If it is your cat that has to travel however, then you need to make the journey as comfortable as possible. Unlike humans, cats will simply not tolerate flights where they are jammed in like sardines.

Travel carriers for kitties should be strong sturdy and roughly equivalent to a human first class seat; with enough room for a fluff ball to lie down, stretch out, turn around and scratch its self. If the flight is a long haul flight, it should also have an absorbent liner, and a provision for water. Popping a blanket, towel or even a t-shirt that has your smell on it will go along way to easing your kitty's distress.

There are quite a few companies that specialize in pet transport, and I highly recommend using one if you are travelling on a plane, especially overseas. Reputable companies will have provisions for watering and caring for your fluffy one in transit, and will be able to guide you through any quarantine and vaccination regulations you need to comply with. They also know which carriers are the most pet friendly and will treat Her Majesty with respect she deserves. I have used JetPets and found them excellent.

FEEDING

As far as feeding is concerned your cat will be endlessly frustrated by your inability to adhere to the simplest of telepathically transmitted commands. It is not their fault that you are unable to understand. They did their part. They sat there, fully focused and beamed you their breakfast order, and you are just too stupid to understand it. Tuna is not salmon! I mean really, how hard is that?

As far as your cat is concerned variety is the spice of life. Just because your cat liked salmon yesterday, you cannot assume that she will condescend to eating it ever again.

While it may seem impossible to adequately cater to your feline's mercurial preferences, the safest strategy is to keep a range of options on hand. Given a selection of fresh meats, tins and pouches and the very occasional high quality cat biscuit, most cats will manage to find something they consider vaguely edible.

Fresh Meat

Cats are natural carnivores and do not tolerate a vegetarian diet. I cannot stress this too heavily. Removing meat from a cat's diet will kill the cat, so if you feel you really can't feed your cat meat, you need to find a new home for him.

Fresh meat will always be the best option for your cat's health, so if it is readily accessible and your cat likes it, this is definitely the way to go.

If getting fresh meat every day is not convenient, meat can be purchased in bulk, divided into portions and frozen at -4oF. Most fresh meats can be stored for several months in the freezer and thawed just prior to use, taking care to follow safe meat-handling procedures at all times).

There is quite a variety of fresh meat that cats enjoy, such as chicken, rabbit, lamb, beef, kangaroo, venison and all kinds of fish.

While cooked bones are definitely off the menu, raw chicken wings, necks and drumsticks are totally fabulous! Most cats totally LOVE them. Be warned though, a drumstick is not just a meal, it is also a toy to be pawed, nudged, tossed around and dragged onto the nearest piece of carpet. For some rather inexplicable reason a drumstick is much better eating when it has been rolled on a rug. (Our cats Mauser and Podge won't even eat their drumsticks until they have been thoroughly converted to what we now call "rug meat").

Cat Biscuits

There is no doubt cat biscuits are very convenient, but there is some debate about whether they are actually harmful to our kitties. While cat biscuits are made primarily from rendered meat products, many brands contain grains and cereals, which are not a part of your cat's natural diet.

There are also lingering questions regarding the quality of the ingredients used in rendered meat products, and most brands produced in the USA and Canada contain genetically modified ingredients.

From the cheapest of supermarket brands through to some very expensive "designer" vet brands, there are many formulations that have special qualities like "dental health", or "hair ball" etc. printed on the package. However this is no guarantee that they will actually assist with such conditions (especially in the cheaper brands). In many cases it simply means a marketing person has decided to put words like dental, or hairball on the pack.

Of course Mauser and Podge just love their biscuits, but we try to keep to quality brands and only give them to them occasionally as special treat, (the high level of carbs really don't help Podge keep his weight in check).

I definitely do not recommend feeding your cat solely on cat biscuits, as it can lead to a range of nasty health problems including:

Diabetes, Chronic Vomiting, Chronic Diarrhoea, High Blood Pressure, Skin and Coat Problems, Inflammatory Bowel Disease, Hepatic Lipidosis (Liver Failure), Heart Disease, Asthma, Allergic Skin Disease, Pancreatitis, Arthritis, Bladder Disease and Kidney Disease.

Biscuits can also be very dehydrating so if you feed your cat a diet high in biscuits you will have to be extra zealous with the water. Cats usually get most of their required moisture from the food they eat, but with dry food that is simply not possible and they will need a lot more water to make up the balance.

Cats do not like standing water, as the dust that gathers on the surface seems to bother them. They like their water very fresh, which is why you often see them licking a recently used basin or shower, or even dunking their heads under a running tap. If you find you forget to change their water with every meal you can invest in a small water fountain that keeps cycling the water so it remains fresh and dust free.

If you must feed your cat dry food, take extra care to keep it dry. Never mix it with canned food, milk, broth, or water. All dried foods have some level of bacterial contamination on the surface, and any moisture present will allow those bacteria to grow. Some common bacteria can be quite dangerous, and can cause vomiting and/or diarrhea.

Never feed your cat the "semi-moist" type foods, as they are full of preservatives, colorings, texturizers, and additives.

If you are using a high percentage of dried food you should change brands (or at the very least flavors) every 2 to 3 months to avoid any possible dietary deficiencies or excesses, which could cause problems for your kitty. However when you are changing kitty's foods, GO SLOWLY. Add a small amount of the new food to the old, and gradually increase the proportion over a period of about a week or two. This will avoid any potential shock to the cat's digestive system, and will also reduce the likelihood of an allergic reaction.

Cats who are diabetic, overweight, or have any history of liver, pancreas, bladder or kidney disease, should not be given any dry or semi-moist food at all.

The low moisture and high carbohydrate content of dried foods is known to exacerbate these problems.

Tins and Pouches

Tins and pouches of cat food are often considered a convenient option as they can be stored in the cupboard.

While good quality tinned wet food is certainly a better option than cat biscuits, it is often significantly more expensive than fresh meat and nowhere near as healthy for your cat. Although they may not be perfect brands promoted as "natural" are generally a better choice; however a quick read of the label can be a real eye opener.

One thing you will commonly find listed in the ingredients of cheaper store brands (and even in some high priced premium and vet brands), is "animal bi-products" (sometimes listed as just "bi-products").

Basically bi-products are any part of the animal other than the meat. That could include things like beaks, feet, lungs, spleen, etc. While a cat in the wild would eat all the by products as well as the meat, the meat would make up the bulk of their diet, whereas animal by-products found in canned foods, are often the sole source of animal protein.

When choosing a commercial cat food always read the label.

Avoid products containing "by-product meal," or "meat and bone meal," which tend to be the cheapest, poorest quality animal-sourced ingredients. MBM (Meat and bone meal) refers to mammal product whereas "by-product meal" refers to poultry. In a study conducted by the US FDA, MBM was flagged as the ingredient most likely to contain the veterinary euthanasia drug sodium pentobarbital, which is not something you want to give your kitty, even in trace amounts.

A specified meat or meat meal should be the main protein source, (not cereals like corn gluten meal). Any form of corn should be avoided, as low-grade corn used in pet food is most likely genetically modified (especially in the USA and Canada). In lower priced foods, corn gluten meal is often used instead of more expensive meat ingredients. Wheat and corn are common allergens, and like all grains wheat and corn are highly susceptible to mould and other toxins; so wheat and corn products should also be avoided where possible.

Many cat food brands are now preserved with Vitamins C and E instead of potentially toxic chemical preservatives. With a little research you can effectively avoid cat foods containing chemical preservatives such as BHT, BHA, ethoxyquin, propylene glycol, or propyl gallate. Although some synthetic preservatives may be present in vitamin preserved brands, the amount will be considerably less.

Stay away from "special formula", "light" or "senior" foods. Many of these foods contain inadequate fats, excessive fiber and acidifying agents that can lead to skin and coat problems.

Generic or store brands should be avoided if possible. They often contain poorer quality ingredients, and may in fact be repackaged rejects from the big manufactures.

While it is preferable for cats to have 100% wet food, they should never have less than 50% of their total food intake in wet food. What ever you feed your kitty it should include a good deal of variety to prevent food intolerances and allergies and to discourage them becoming from becoming finicky or fussy eaters.

Fat Cats

Feline obesity has become an increasing problem in recent years. It brings with it many health risks for your oversized fur ball. Apart

from the general discomfort of lugging around all that extra weight, they can suffer arthritis, cardio vascular problems, diabetes, hepatic liver and kidney problems etc.

The biggest culprits in the epidemic of obese kitties (apart from our inability to say no to that adorable beggy faced feline) are dried cat biscuits.

Many brands of cat biscuits contain high levels of grains, something that is not present in a cat's natural diet. Grains, being carbohydrates, push insulin levels up beyond what cats would normally experience on a pure protein diet; this spike in insulin leads to a decrease in activity and an increase in appetite, resulting in a tsunami of fat cats.

We are doing our little fluffy ones no favors by indulging their whims, and we may in fact be dramatically shortening their lives.

All cats need grass.

All cats love to munch on grass. Even though it often makes them throw up, they seem to find the odd nibble on a blade of grass irresistible. While no one has managed to definitely ascertain why cats feel so compelled to munch on the lawn, experts have come up with a few likely reasons.

As carnivores cats often ingest both the edible and inedible parts of their pray, such as fur, bones and feathers. Some theorize that

as grass makes cats regurgitate (due to the fact that they lack the enzymes necessary to digest it), grass is an effective way for cats to clear these indigestible irritants from their digestive tracts.

Another popular theory is that grass munching is triggered by a cat's need for folic acid. Folic acid is essential for a cat's overall health, and assists in the production of haemoglobin.

Then there is the laxative theory. While we all know cats like to throw up fur balls, but sometimes if the hair has moved a little further down the digestive tract, kitty may need a little extra fibre to move it out the other end.

Whatever the reason, cats seem to know that they need to eat a little grass now and again to keep themselves healthy; and if you have an indoor cat that means growing a pot or tray of cat grass or cat nip. It's really very easy to do and can be purchased quite inexpensively from your local garden centre.

OCCASIONAL TREATS

There are a number of foods that most cats love, but unfortunately are not all that good for them. Many of these foods have some small level of risk or minor side effect that you should consider before popping such treats on the menu.

Milk and Other Dairy Products

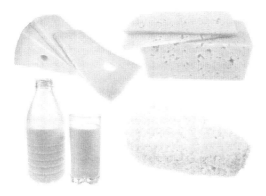

Some cats will go crazy for a saucer of milk or a piece of cheese, but the trouble is most cats are lactose-intolerant. Their digestive systems simply cannot process dairy foods, and consuming dairy can leave your cat with digestive upset or diarrhoea. If your cat just loves milk, you can give him the occasional drink of lactose free milk as a safer alternative.

Liver

Cat's LOVE liver, but eating too much liver can cause vitamin A toxicity. Small amounts of liver are OK, but vitamin A toxicity is a serious condition and can cause death. It can also affect your cat's bones. Symptoms include osteoporosis, deformed bones and bone growths on the elbows and spine.

Tuna

Many cats love tuna and will joyfully chow down on it at every meal. While the occasional feast of tuna is not a problem, too much tuna is simply not good for cats. Regardless of whether it's packed for cats or for humans you need to keep it no more than about one meal every few days. Human tuna will not have all the nutrients your cat needs to be healthy, and cat tuna may contain grains, fillers and preservatives that you are trying to avoid. Too much tuna can also cause mercury poisoning.

Raw Eggs

A small amount of raw egg occasionally is unlikely to harm your kitty, but there are a couple of very real potential problems. The first is the possibility of bacteria like salmonella or E. coli causing food poisoning. (Although this is also a potential problem for humans who eat raw eggs too). The second is that avidin, a protein found in raw egg whites, can interfere with the absorption of some B group vitamins, which can cause skin problems as well as problems with your cat's coat. If you are confident the eggs are fresh and bacterial contamination is not a risk then a small occasional amount of egg white won't hurt them, but it is a risk and definitely not something to make a regular habit of.

STRICTLY OFF THE MENU!

Alcohol

Pound for pound it takes far less alcohol to damage a cat than it does to damage a human. As little as two teaspoons of whisky can put a five pound cat into a coma, three teaspoons could easily kill it. Never give your cat alcohol!

Caffeine

Large quantities of caffeine can be fatal for cats; and there is no antidote for caffeine poisoning. Symptoms include rapid breathing, heart palpitations, restlessness, muscle tremors, and fits. Tea and coffee are not the only sources of caffeine, it can also be found in chocolate, sodas, cocoa, and so called "energy" drinks like Red Bull. It's also in some cold medicines and painkillers. The good news is a cat will never consume this by its own choice, but there is a definite risk when giving cats human medicines.

Chocolate

There is no subtle way to say this; chocolate can kill your cat! Theobromine, the toxic agent in chocolate, can also cause nasty seizures, tremors and abnormal heart rhythm. All kinds of chocolate contain theobromine, even white chocolate, but the most dangerous varieties are dark chocolate and unsweetened baking chocolate. Although most cats won't eat chocolate on their own, they can be coaxed into eating it.

Onions, Chives and Garlic

Onions, garlic and chives can cause gastrointestinal upset in cats. Onion, be it cooked, raw, powdered, or dehydrated, can break down a cat's red blood cells, leading to anemia. While a small dose occasionally probably won't hurt your kitty, a large quantity once or regularly eating smaller amounts can cause onion poisoning. Most cats will only ingest onion when they are fed meat based human food scraps, so take care when feeding kitty your left overs.

Your Medicine

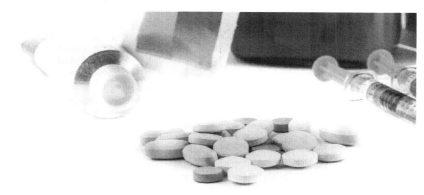

Human medicines account for the vast majority of cat poisonings. The best precautions are to keep all medicines where your cat can't get to them, and never give your cat any over-the-counter human medicine unless your vet specifically advises you to do so. Common ingredients in human medicines, like acetaminophen or ibuprofen, can be deadly for your cat.

Cooked Bones

*NO COOKED BONES!!! NOT EVER!!! While chewing meat off raw bones is good for your cat's teeth and jaws, cooked bones can become brittle and splinter, lodging in your cat's throat. If this

occurs your cat will probably require expensive surgery and may not survive. Chicken bones are the worst offenders. If you are eating cooked meat with bones be sure to clean up immediately after you have finished. Do not leave plates with bones lying on the sink where your cat can get at them.

Grapes and Raisins

Cats have been known to eat grapes and raisins if they find them lying around, but they are really not good for kitties. Grapes and raisins can cause kidney failure and even a small amount can lead to vomiting and hyperactivity. While some cats seem unaffected it's better not to take that risk. Take care to keep them off countertops where you cat can get to them.

Xylitol - Candies and Gums

Many common diet foods, toothpastes, baked goods, gums and candies are sweetened with Xylitol. Xylitol can spike your cat's insulin levels, which can cause an extreme drop in blood sugar. Xylitol can also lead to liver failure, with symptoms include lethargy, loss of coordination and vomiting, The cat may have seizures soon after ingesting the xylitol, and liver failure can occur within just a few days.

HEALTH AND HYGIENE

Going to the vet

Our cat Mauser thinks that every time we get in the car we are off to the vets. Which kind of makes sense to her because every time she gets in the car we go to that place with the steel table, rectal thermometers and that really yummy brand of cat food. She thinks we regularly subject ourselves to gum inspections, sharp injections, and having our temperatures taken via our rear ends, just to get that delicious cat food for her. Naturally this only enhances her love for us.

I don't care what the anti-vaxers say; your cat needs its shots! There is cat AIDS out there, and your cat can catch it from just the scratch of an infected cat. There is also cat flu and a range of other diseases that can be effectively immunized against.

No-one likes going to the doctor, especially your cat, but like all of us your cat needs to get an annual check up.

Common Cat Ailments:

Hairballs

When cats groom themselves they automatically swallow a certain amount of loose hair. On occasions this hair will form a ball that lodges in the cat's digestive tract, which causes the cat to try and cough up or vomit out the offending object.

The odd hairball every now and then isn't really a problem, but if kitty is hacking up fuzzballs more than once or twice a month it is time to take action.

First thing is a trip to the vet to make sure the problem really is hairballs and not something more serious. Constant coughing and hacking but no hair balls coming up can be a sign of kitty asthma.

Prevention is the best strategy for dealing with hairballs. If your cat is particularly susceptible you will need to brush His Majesty regularly to remove any dead or loose hair. If brushing is not as effective as you might wish you may need to upgrade to a fine tooth flea comb, although some cats may take a while to get used to and accept combing.

Many cats that suffer hairballs will attempt to self medicate by eating grass. Being unable to digest the grass the cat will then throw up, and with any luck the offending hairball will come with it. If your kitty's initial attempts to hack up the hairball are unsuccessful you may need to look beyond just grass and add a lubricant to the digestive tract to help ease the hairball out the other end.

The cheapest, and one of the most highly effective lubricants for the job is plain simple Vaseline. The molecules in Vaseline are far too large to be absorbed by the cat's intestines, and it will pass directly through to cat perfectly safely. However getting the Vaseline actually into the cat is not always easy. You could try forcing feeding it to your cat with a syringe but you may come off worse for the encounter. One of the most effective ways to administer it is to smear a couple of small blobs on her front paws.

If the idea of trying to get Vaseline into your cat is a bit much for you there are also a number of commercial products specifically designed for the task, such as Laxatone, Petromalt, or Katalax. These usually come flavored with tuna or liver, and cats generally find them palatable.

Worms

Worm infestation is not uncommon in cats, but fortunately they are easily treated with worming tablets. While tapeworms, roundworms and hookworms are the most common cats are also susceptible to heartworm.

The symptoms can include weight loss, poor coat appearance vomiting and a pot bellied appearance. If you suspect your cat has worms you should take him to the vet immediately. If left untreated worms can cause serious health problems.

Vomiting

There can many reasons why a cat may vomit, from hairballs, worms, eating grass or plants, food intolerances, eating too quickly, overeating, changes in diet, eating food that has gone off to eating birds, rodents, lizards or other wild life.

An occasional upchuck is quite normal and not usually a sign of anything too sinister. However if your cat has chronic, severe or persistent vomiting then you need to get him to the vet for a check up. Vomiting in cats can be a sign of a serious underlying disorder, so try to provide your vet with as good a picture as possible of your cat's general health. Does your cat have any other symptoms like diarrhoea or loss of appetite? Is he lethargic? Is there any chance he could have been poisoned?

Diarrhoea

While diarrhoea is not a disease in and of itself, it is a sign that something is not quite right with your kitty's health. Diarrhoea is most often a minor problem, but it could also signify a more serious illness.

If your fluffy one has other symptoms, such as loss of appetite, dehydration, fever, pain, lethargy, weight loss, depression, or foul smelling faeces you should take her to the vet immediately to rule out any potentially serious illness.

The prime suspect when looking for the cause of kitty diarrhoea is the contents of her food bowl. Obviously what she eats is going to affect the quality of her poo! Often the culprit is in cheaper brands of cat food that are bulked out with grains or vegetables or other carbohydrates that are would not normally form part of your cat's diet, and may pass through her like an express train.

As a basic rule of thumb I would feed your cat the best quality food that you can afford.

If your cat is showing signs of diarrhoea but otherwise seems healthy you could try withholding food for 24 hours (12 hours for kittens), to give the cat's digestive tract a bit of break, then resume feeding a diet of unprocessed bland meat, (such as chicken or cooked mince) for a few days. Avoid dairy, dry or processed foods. If the situation doesn't resolve within a day or so, then it is off to see the vet.

Cats suffering from diarrhoea can lose a lot of water, so you need to keep an extra eye out for dehydration. You can check your cat's hydration level by gently pulling up a fold of skin on the cat's back. When you let go the skin should rapidly return to its natural position. If the skin is slow to return to its normal position this is a sign of dehydration.

While you can encourage your cat to drink water, if your cat is dehydrated you may want to give her "Lectade". "Lectade" is an oral re-hydration therapy for cats. It is excellent for reversing the effects of electrolyte loss and dehydration in cats after a bout of diarrhoea.

Urinary Tract Infections

Bladder problems are a much feared but relatively uncommon health issue in cats. Feline lower urinary tract disorders (often referred to as LUTD, FLUTD, or FUS--feline urologic syndrome), come in a number of distinct varieties, but all together they affect less than 3% of cats.

Urinary tract infections affect both male and female cats, however male cats are at a significantly higher risk of life-threatening blockages of the urethra, with the condition usually developing between the ages 2 and 7, (although it can also occur in very old or very young cats). External stressors, such as moving home, disruptive renovations, severe weather, or the loss or addition of a family member, can trigger episodes of FLUTD.

Frequent urination, straining to urinate, passing only very small amounts of urine at a time, licking their genitals more often and more intensely than usual, and having blood in the urine are all symptoms of FLUTDs. Sometimes cats with FLUTDs mistakenly associate the litter box with the burning pain of their condition and look for another place to go where it won't hurt. This can lead cats urinating in corners, sinks, on carpets or rugs, in laundry baskets or beds.

If you suspect your cat has an FLUTD it is important to get them to the vet as soon as possible, as it can lead to a blockage of the urinary tract. If a blockage occurs the toxins backed up in the urine can lead to kidney failure and death within 24 hours.

Cystitis and Bladder Stones

Roughly two thirds of all FLUTDs are what is called "idiopathic cystitis", which simply means an inflammation of the bladder of cause unknown. Cystitis can occasionally be caused by serious conditions such as kidney stones, defects in the bladder wall, bladder cancer or other systemic diseases. Bacteria is rarely a causal factor.

In about 20% of cases bladder or kidney stones are present. Some stones can be dissolved and dislodged by diet, though it can take an excessively long time; often having them surgically removed is the best option. If a cat exhibits signs of an FLUTD that last more than a week in spite of treatment, he should be given an ultra sound or X-ray to check for stones or any other possible anatomic abnormalities.

Diet for FLUTD

There are a number of special diet foods for cats that are designed to dissolve stones and to prevent them reoccurring; including, Purina CNM-UR, Hill's s/d, c/d(s) and c/d(o), Waltham's Control pHormula, and others. These create acid-base conditions in the cat's body that help to dissolve the stones, but should be monitored regularly by your vet. Canned versions of these foods are far preferable to dry, with studies suggesting that cats on the canned varieties remained 90% symptom free after one year, compared to only 60% of cats on the dry food. Dry cat foods are known to carry a higher risk of dehydration and high urine concentration, therefore cats with FLUTDs should not be fed dry food if it at all possible.

Fleas

Many people don't consider a few fleas to be a serious issue, but they can be quite damaging to your cat's health. Fleas bite their host in order to feed on its blood; heavy infestations can cause cats to become anaemic, and they even have been known to kill kittens. Fleas can also spread tapeworm from one animal to another.

Some cats are quite allergic to flea saliva which can lead to constant scratching, and aggravated skin problems. The most common allergy dermatitis in cats and dogs is a flea allergy.

There are a number of treatments for fleas, such as collars, baths, and spot on medications, however fleas can be a stubborn pest and it can take several months of vigilance to break their breeding cycle and kill all their eggs. While you are dealing with a flea problem regular vacuuming is essential to remove any eggs from your carpets and you may even need to remove the family and pets for a few hours and let off some flea bombs.

Conjunctivitis

Conjunctivitis, (inflammation of the membranes around the eye) can be a chronic problem for some cats. The eye may appear red, swollen, weepy and crusty or any combination of the above. Persistent squinting and excessive blinking may also be indicators of infection.

Conjunctivitis is often a secondary condition resulting from another infection, which may be either viral or bacterial. There are a number of common infections that can lead to conjunctivitis including:

1. Feline Herpes virus (FHV-1 often referred to as Cat Flu)

2. Feline Chlamydophila. (Formerly known as Chlamydia)

3. Feline Calicivirus (FCV often referred to as Cat Flu).

Viral eye infections are often accompanied by secondary bacterial infections, which are treated with an antibiotic ointment or oral treatment.

There are a number of other potential causes such as allergies, injury, foreign objects in the eye or congenital defects such as small tear ducts.

Persians cats are particularly prone to hereditary eye conditions and often suffer chronic infections that result in excess tearing and discomfort.

Bathing the eyes in a saline solution is a soothing treatment for kitty conjunctivitis that you can administer at home. This helps relieve irritation and is useful for washing out viral particles from the eye. You can also use it to remove any crusts of mucus from the eye.

Add one quarter of a teaspoon of table salt to one cup of water and mix well. Soak a cotton ball in the solution and use it to drip a small amount of the solution into the cat's eyes. You can also gently wipe the crust or seepage from the cat's eye (if the cat will allow it). Bathe the cat's eyes 3 or 4 times a day, making sure to use fresh solution and cotton balls for each session.

I strongly recommend that you consult your veterinarian for a definite diagnosis for all eye problems.

Feline Leukaemia Virus

Until recently FLV was the most common fatal disease of cats, however the recent development of an effective vaccine has seen a huge drop off in reported cases. The FLV vaccine should be on your kitty's list of regular top up vaccinations.

Although the name leukaemia usually means cancer of the white blood cells, there are a number of other diseases associated with this virus, such as anaemia, arthritis, respiratory infections and other types of cancer.

While FLV is not always immediately fatal, infected cats usually have a significantly reduced life expectancy. You should NEVER bring other cats into your household when you have a cat with FLV, especially ones that are not vaccinated.

Lyme Disease

If your cat spends a lot of time outdoors, you should check him regularly for ticks. Ticks carry Lyme disease, so if your cat has been exposed to tick bites and is lethargic or acting like he is in pain get your vet to test for Lyme disease.

Some cats may have no symptoms at all whereas others show only the mildest of symptoms. Lyme disease can be hard to recognize and it is often mistaken for other illnesses or old age. Often no tick is found, so if you live in a tic prone area it is best to keep a sharp eye on your kitty's behaviour.

Symptoms of Feline Lyme Disease include lethargy, loss of appetite, reluctance to climb stairs or jump, limping and a reluctance to put weight on a paw.

Prevention, early diagnosis and quick treatment are by far the best ways of dealing with Feline Lyme Disease. If at all possible you should take measures to reduce the tick population around your home.

Abscesses

Bites or scratches from other cats are the most common cause of feline abscesses. Cats have tough leathery skin that doesn't tear easily, which means that teeth and claws very often don't leave any significant visible surface wounds. Instead they tend to penetrate deeply into the muscle tissue, lodging any bacteria or foreign body present well beneath the skin. The small puncture wounds tend to heal over very quickly, trapping any bacteria, which thrives in the warm, moist environment. The build up of bacteria leads to the painful accumulation of pus under the skin we know as an abscess.

Initially your cat may not show any overt signs of distress, but between two to five days after a fight he may start to exhibit the characteristic soft painful swelling under the skin, and as the infection takes hold he may develop lethargy, fever and loss of appetite. Blood poisoning can even occur as the release of bacteria toxins and the by products of dying tissue enters the blood stream. It is no exaggeration to say a cat with an abscess can become quite ill.

Symptoms of cat abscess

A cat with an abscess is a cat in a great deal of pain. Any combination of the following may indicate your cat has an abscess:

any lumps or hot inflamed areas

sudden loss of appetite.

reluctance to move or play

fever

limping

reluctance to betouched

Treating an abscess

Sometime an abscess will rupture spontaneously, releasing a thick, foul smelling, brown or yellow pus. This usually results in the cat feeling a lot better and resuming its normal eating regime.

If your cat will allow it you can clip away the fur near the wound and gently wash away any discharge or scabs with warm salty water. The more discharge you can remove the better.

If the abscess does not rupture on its own within a day or two you

110

will need to have it surgically drained by the vet. The vet will usually insert a surgical drain to allow further discharge to occur over the next few days. If this is done your cat may be fitted with a collar for a couple of days to stop him chewing and aggravating the area. Antibiotics are usually prescribed to clear up any remaining bacterial infection and the vet will remove the drain after a few days.

Our cat Mauser used to get bullied quite a bit, and would often come home with bites and scratches. She tended to go down hard when she had been attacked by other cats, and we learnt very quickly that it was best to take her to the vet immediately we noticed she had been in a fight. By starting her on a course of antibiotics immediately we managed to avoid many abscesses and their expensive complications.

After a catfight, you should check your cat for any painful areas and puncture wounds, paying particular attention to the head, neck and forelegs, and the lower back at the base of the spine. Like our lovely Mauser, many cats will be injured on their rear as they flee from their attacker. Look for any tufts of matted hair, scabs or clotted blood. Do not dismiss small scratches or holes as insignificant. Apply gentle pressure to any suspect site and check the cat's reaction for pain. Repeat this again the next day taking careful note of any increase in pain levels.

Keeping your cat inside at night and neutering male cats will reduce the frequency and severity of fights.

Dental Problems

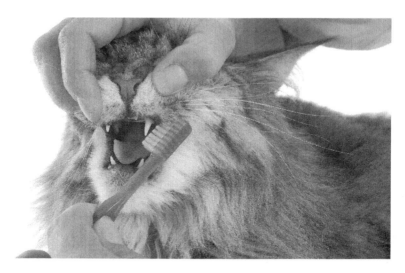

The most common feline dental issue is a condition called Feline odontoclastic resorptive lesions (FORL). While FORL can vary quite a bit in severity it can be absolutely excruciating for kitties. Often an effected cat will stop eating and drinking. They may attempt to eat but drop the food as it is too painful to chew. A cat with FORL may also drool excessively, have bleeding from the mouth and have really nasty breath. He may paw at his mouth or flinch in pain when you go anywhere near his mouth region. A simple tooth extraction at the vet will usually fix the problem and have your cat back on top in no time.

While FORL is the most common cause of dental issues there are a number of other issues that can cause mouth pain for kitties. These include abscessed or broken teeth, mouth tumors, inflammation of the gums (also known as gingivitis), periodontitis (inflammation of the soft tissue surrounding the teeth, bones or other foreign bodies stuck between the teeth, kidney disease and feline leukemia virus.

While cat's breath is not generally the most pleasant smell on the planet (and certainly no-one has attempted to market a perfume based on it), when your cat gets ill its breath can smell particularly foul. Bad breath in cats can be a sign of chronic renal failure, so if you are reeling at the slightest whiff, it's off to the vet.

Kidney failure

The body uses food for energy and self repair, and after the body has taken what it needs from the food, waste is sent to the blood and transported to the kidneys, which are basically a filtering system. Kitty's kidneys are surprisingly resilient. It is often not until your cat has lost about 70% of kidney function that any problems become apparent. Once kidney function is seriously impaired and the kidneys are unable to remove enough of the waste toxins build up in the system, which leads to systemic poisoning. It can also cause other problems such as anemia, high blood pressure and bone disease.

Kidney failure is usually a progressive condition, where the deterioration occurs over a long period of time. Kidney failure is one of the most common causes of death in older cats.

Symptoms of kidney disease include decreased appetite, increased thirst and urination, weight loss, drooling, lethargy, bad breath, poor coat condition, vomiting and anemia.

Chronic renal failure is an irreversible condition but with proper treatment a cat may have many months or years of life ahead. Fresh drinking water is extremely important as they will need to make up for the fluids lost through frequent urination. Fluids are also required to keep the toxins flushed out of kitty's system. Sometimes a vet will administer subcutaneous fluids to treat dehydration and electrolyte imbalances. Your cat will require a specialized prescription diet with a lower proportion of phosphorous and protein than normal cat food.

Feline Diabetes

There are two types of diabetes that affect our feline friends. Type one, where the pancreas doesn't produce enough insulin; and type two where the body's cells don't respond properly to insulin. Much the same in cats as it is in humans the vast majority of feline sufferers have type two diabetes.

Symptoms range from increased thirst and appetite, weight loss, weakness in the hind legs, bad breath, poor coat condition, vomiting, increased urination and lethargy. Depending on the severity of the condition you may not see all of these symptoms.

Type one sufferers may be required to have daily insulin injections, type two sufferers may also require injections but may be improved with diet. If the condition is properly managed a cat with diabetes can expect to live for many years.

THE LITTER BOX

One of the most vexing problems for cat carers is kitty "going outside the box". There are however a number of proactive things you can do to minimize the chances of this occurring.

Keep it clean

The cardinal rule of the litter box is keep it clean please!! And don't try using any of those gimmicky self cleaning, scent adding products to try to avoid it. I am afraid that if you have an indoor cat you just have to suck it up; properly cleaning the litter tray is in the job description!!

Cats are clean fastidious animals and that is exactly how they like their bathroom facilities. Most times when a cat goes outside the litter box it is because the litter tray is simply not clean.

If you can imagine being offered the use of a toilet that had not been flushed for a week, surely you too would seek out somewhere else to go? Have you ever found yourself thinking "oh goody a porta-potty...I LOVE them"? No, didn't think so! What's more, would you tolerate being asked to walk around in your own excreta to relieve yourself? Well that is what you are asking your cat to do if you fail to keep the litter box clean. Cats have an extraordinarily sensitive sense of smell, so if you think how unappealing we would find the smell of a well used, unflushed toilet and magnify that by 100 times, well you get the picture. Basically ....eeeewwww!

*(There are several serious medical reasons a cat may stop using the litter tray so if this happens after you have cleaned the tray and the area, or happens more than once take kitty to see the vet immediately).

You should scoop feces out of the litter box daily. How frequently you should replace the litter depends on the number factors, such as how many cats and how many litter boxes, and of course the type of litter.

As a general guideline you should look at once every three to four days for replacing clay litter. However you may need to replace it every second day, or as little as once a week, depending on the circumstances.

Clumping litter will often go a bit longer between changes. If you clean the litter box every day you may only need to change it once every two to three weeks. However if you notice any odors or if a good proportion of the litter is wet or clumped, it needs to be changed.

Scrub the tray using a mild dish detergent every time you change the litter and avoid using products with ammonia or citrus oils as they can turn a cat off. Some cleaning products can be toxic to cats so sticking with mild dish detergent is by far the easiest and safest option.

Location, location

There is a tendency for cat carers to want to put the litter box in some out of the way spot, as this will keep the odour down and reduce the trail of litter box footprints that are marched through the house. However just like you wouldn't want to go to the bathroom in the basement or on a cold damp concrete floor your cat may be less than impressed if you ask them to do it in such unpleasant places; and if the box is too out of the way for a kitten or elderly cat to make it, they simply may not use it.

Fortunately there is usually some level of compromise that can be struck that you both can live with. Try keeping the litter box in a spot that gives the cat some privacy, but is not too hard to get to. Do not place it too close to a heater as this can amplify the smell, which can be a turn off for a cat, and avoid placing it near a noisy appliance as this may startle the cat and make it too nervous to use the box.

Keep the litter box well away from food and water bowls. Like us cats don't like to mix the in and the out!

Place a litter box for each cat on every level of the house. That way your cat should always have access to a box even if there is a shut door, If you have a single story home, and multiple cats try to have litter trays in at least two places, this will help prevent your cats ambushing each other while in "motion".

If you keep a litter tray in a cupboard or a bathroom, be sure the door is wedged open from both sides to stop your cat from getting locked out or stuck inside.

Pick of the litter

There are many different types of cat litter on the market, including traditional clay litter, scooping or clumping litter, crystal-based silica gel litter and plant-derived bio-degradable litter.

Most cats prefer fine-grained litters, as they tend to have a softer feel. Clumping and silica gel based litters are usually fine grained and thus tend to be better received than your typical clay litter; and as an added bonus they tend to keep the odor under control a bit more effectively.

That said there are some high-quality, dust-free clay litters that are fairly small-grained and may be quite acceptable to your cat.

If you have an outdoor cat that is now an indoor cat you may need to put river pebbles or rocks in the base of your pot plants to keep kitty from thinking of them as indoor toilets. If your cat rejects all commercial litters it may accept a sand box.

There is a certain amount of trial and error in finding just the right litter for your cat, but once you find one she is happy with it is best to stick with it. Changing your brand of litter too often may result in kitty going outside the box.

What is that smell?

Scented litters can actually repel some cats, so generally try to avoid them. Cats can also be put off or disturbed by room deodorizers or air fresheners near their litter box. The best strategy for keeping the smell down is to clean the box regularly and add a thin layer of baking soda to the bottom of the box before adding fresh litter. Baking soda is excellent at absorbing odors and it will not repel your cat.

Under cover

Some folks like to use covered litter boxes, but this is not always the cat's preference. If you are unsure whether your cat is happy with a covered box, try using one covered and one uncovered and see which one he is drawn to.

Covered boxes often reduce the amount of stray litter particles and mess around the box, but they can also amplify the smell of the box for your cat, which may cause your cat to look for another alternative. If you are using a covered box you may want to keep it extra clean to keep kitty happy going in there.

There are a few other issues with covered boxes. For example it is easy to forget to change the litter as often as required. The box may not have enough room for the cat to comfortably dig and scratch and position himself, which makes it a lot easier for cats to ambush each other as they exit the box. All of these things can have your cat seeking out your pot plants, or worse.

How deep is your litter?

Ok, it is not a happy truth, but more litter in the tray does not mean less frequent cleaning. If you have more than two inches of litter in the tray a lot of cats will not use it. In fact there are longhaired cats that actually prefer less litter so that they can reach the bottom of the tray easily.

Litter problems?

If your cat starts to go outside the litter box with any regularity you should consult the vet immediately, as many serious health problems are first identified through a change in litter box behaviour.

If your cat is given the all clear by the vet it is possible there is a physical problem with the box. It may be that the box is not clean enough or that cats are ambushing each other at the box. It could even be that the box is too far away, or not in the right place for some reason.

Once you have fixed any potential box problems the next step is to look at the possibility of intruder cats or some kind of behavioral problem.

Cats will often spray if they feel another cat is encroaching upon their territory. Check to see if there are any other cats using your cat door or gaining access some other way. If a cat doesn't feel that they have a place to call their own they can become very distressed and this can cause toilet problems such as marking. Make sure your cat has a safe space that they identify as belonging only to them.

Banishing your cat outdoors or devising some other sort of punishment is never the answer, this is only likely to make the cat confused and distressed. There is always a reason for the behavior and if you can identify it, it is usually a fairly simply fix. If you feel you have tried everything and are unable to identify a cause it is worth contacting an animal-behavioralist.

CATS AND HUMANS
A LOVE STORY

As it is with so many great love stories, the relationship between cats and humans can be intense, unpredictable and somewhat lopsided. We adore them, we crave their attentions and affections. And while they are prepared to spend a certain amount of time with us, they often leave us with the impression that they think they could do better.

In spite of the obvious power imbalance the relationship has managed to endure for many thousands of years. While it is impossible to say exactly when cats first abandoned their wild ways and bonded us into their service, in 1983 archaeologists on the island of Cyprus found an eight thousand year old feline jawbone. Not being native to Cyprus, and Cyprus being an island it didn't stretch the grey matter too far to conclude that the cat must have been shipped onto the island by some seafaring humans, (either that or they rode there on the backs of gigantic swimming rats).

Given the unlikelihood of a boatload of ancient mariners being prepared to share their vessel with a snarly, bitey, aggressive ball of feral teeth and claws, one could reasonably assume that the cat that came over on the boat was at least somewhat domesticated.

Then in 2004 they discovered a cat that had been deliberately buried beside a human, a discovery that indicated feline domestication had taken place at least fifteen hundred years earlier, which puts domestic cats in Cyprus almost ten thousand years ago.

A study published in the Journal of Science postulates that all domestic cats descended from the Middle Eastern wildcat, Felis sylvestris, (which literally means "cat of the woods.") with the study's authors speculating that the process began up to 12,000 years ago.

Cats and Human Civilization

It was about twelve thousand years ago that agricultural societies began to pop up in the Middle East's fertile crescent. This is no idle coincidence.

Those canny cats understood what exactly the humans were up to. By planting and storing grain in confined spaces they had created a method of concentrating rodent populations in storehouses around their settlements. Ingenious!

Wild cats, that had up until that time relied solely on roaming far and wide to hunt enough food, could now lazily loll about the human villages, and pick off mice at their leisure. Of course this worked wonderfully well for the humans, who for some inexplicable reason seemed to have the mice dealt with.

With all those tasty mice on offer the cats just wandered in and made themselves right at home. With over ninety million cats in the USA today it is estimated that up to half of the USA's human population is engaged in some level of cat service.

THE CAT THROUGHOUT HISTORY

Gods and Demons

While the love has endured, that isn't to say the cat human relationship hasn't been through times of extreme ambivalence. Humans have held cats to be both gods and demons at various points in history.

The ancient Egyptians really had their catly priorities sorted. Cats were gods, (why would anybody even question that?); and Bastet, the Egyptian goddess of love had a cat's head. Cats were habitually mummified, (archeologists even found a cat cemetery with over three hundred thousand mummified cats), and killing a cat usually meant a death sentence.

Seen as a symbol of liberty, the ancient Romans revered their cats in a slightly more secular way; and in the Far-East cats were eagerly welcomed as the defenders of precious manuscripts, which were otherwise subject to rodent attack.

Europe in the middle ages was a bit of a challenging time for kitties. For some reason, cats became totally demonized. They were seen as little furry devils, or witches' familiars and many were killed in an ignorant attempt to ward off evil. Of course humans were duly punished for their folly; for had they not killed all those kitties, the rats that carried the plague across the continent may not have got such a foothold.

Of course things have improved a lot for the fluffy ones since the renaissance age. Cats are now super stars. They star in movies, cartoons and comic strips, they have their own Youtube channels, and cat products and services are a multi billion dollar industry. You can buy your cat anything from a sweater to a pair of sunglasses.

KITTY QUIPS

Cats are, without doubt, the rock stars of the animal world. Everyone, from the most famous to the most humble among us has something to say about cats.

As a fitting farewell I thought I would share some notable kitty quotes with you.

"You see, wire telegraph is a kind of a very, very long cat. You pull his tail in New York and his head is meowing in Los Angeles. Do you understand this? And radio operates exactly the same way: you send signals here, they receive them there. The only difference is that there is no cat."

-*Albert Einstein (theoretical physicist)*

"My relationship with my cats has saved me from a deadly, pervasive ignorance."

-*William S. Burroughs (author)*

"Meow" means "woof" in cat."

-*George Carlin (comedian)*

"It is a very inconvenient habit of kittens (Alice had once made the remark) that, whatever you say to them they always purr."

-*Lewis Carroll (author)*

"Cats choose us; we don't own them."
-*Kristin Cast (author)*

"Those who'll play with cats must expect to be scratched."

-*Miguel de Cervantes (author)*

"I love cats because I enjoy my home; and little by little, they become its visible soul."

-*Jean Cocteau (director)*

132

"Way down deep, we're all motivated by the same urges. Cats have the courage to live by them."

-Jim Davis (cartoonist)

"What greater gift than the love of a cat?"

-Charles Dickens (author)

"Making movies is like herding cats."

-Eric Fellner (movie producer)

"A countryman between two lawyers is like a fish between two cats."

-Benjamin Franklin (Founding Father of the United States)

"Time spent with cats is never wasted."

-*Sigmund Freud (psychoanalyst)*

"If you want to write, keep cats."

-*Aldous Huxley (author)*

"A cat can be trusted to purr when she is pleased, which is more than can be said for human beings."

-*William Ralph Inge (author)*

"Curiosity killed the cat."

-*Ben Johnson (playwright)*

"I used to love dogs until I discovered cats."

-*Nafisa Joseph (model)*

"Cats, like men, are flatterers."

-*Walter Savage Landor (author)*

"The smallest feline is a masterpiece."

-*Leonardo da Vinci (artist)*

"Cats know how to obtain food without labour, shelter without confinement, and love without penalties."

-*Walter Lionel George*

"Cats will outsmart dogs every time."

-*John Grogan*

"How we behave toward cats here below determines our status in heaven."

-*Robert A. Heinlein (author)*

"A cat has absolute emotional honesty: human beings, for one reason or another, may hide their feelings, but a cat does not."

-*Ernest Hemingway (author)*

"Cats are connoisseurs of comfort."

-*James Herriot (author)*

"In its flawless grace and superior self-sufficiency I have seen a symbol of the perfect beauty and bland impersonality of the universe itself, objectively considered, and in its air of silent mystery there resides for me all the wonder and fascination of the unknown."

-H.P. Lovecraft

"Artists like cats; soldiers like dogs."

-Desmond Morris

"Cats do not have to be shown how to have a good time, for they are unfailing ingenious in that respect."

-James Mason

"There are two means of refuge from the miseries of life: music and cats."

-Albert Schweitzer

"I am as vigilant as a cat to steal cream."

-William Shakespeare

"I have studied many philosophers and many cats. The wisdom of cats is infinitely superior."

Hippolyte Taine (critic)

"I have lived with several Zen masters — all of them cats."

-Eckhart Tolle (author)

"Of all God's creatures, there is only one that cannot be made slave of the lash. That one is the cat. If man could be crossed with the cat it would improve the man, but it would deteriorate the cat."

-*Mark Twain (author)*

Cats are smarter than dogs. You can't get eight cats to pull a sled through snow."

-*Jeff Valdez*

"If a dog jumps into your lap it is because he is fond of you; but if a cat does the same thing it is because your lap is warmer."

-*A.N. Whitehead (mathematician and philosopher)*

"The phrase 'domestic cat' is an oxymoron."

-*George Will (columnist)*

"In ancient times cats were worshipped as gods; they have not forgotten this."

-Terry Pratchett (author)

"Women and cats will do as they please, and men and dogs should relax and get used to the idea."

-Robert A. Heinlein (author)

"Cats are very independent animals. They're very sexy, if you want. Dogs are different. They're familiar. They're obedient. You call a cat, you go, 'Cat, come here.' He doesn't come to you unless you have something in your hand that he thinks might be food. They're very free animals, and I like that."

Antonio Banderas (actor)

"I am fond of pigs. Dogs look up to us. Cats look down on us. Pigs treat us as equals."

-Winston Churchill

"Owners of dogs will have noticed that, if you provide them with food and water and shelter and affection, they will think you are God. Whereas owners of cats are compelled to realize that, if you provide them with food and water and affection, they draw the conclusion that they are God."

-Christopher Hitchens (author)

"Cats have it all - admiration, an endless sleep, and company only when they want it."

-Rod McKuen

"As anyone who has ever been around a cat for any length of time well knows, cats have enormous patience with the limitations of the human kind."

-Cleveland Amory

"No matter how much cats fight, there always seem to be plenty of kittens."

-Abraham Lincoln

"I have felt cats rubbing their faces against mine and touching my cheek with claws carefully sheathed. These things, to me, are expressions of love."

-James Herriot (author)

"I like cats a lot. I've always liked cats. They're great company. When they eat, they always leave a little bit at the bottom of the bowl. A dog will polish the bowl, but a cat always leaves a little bit. It's like an offering."

Christopher Walken (actor)

"Just watching my cats can make me happy."

-Paula Cole

"I really am a cat transformed into a woman."

-Brigitte Bardot

"There is no snooze button on a cat who wants breakfast."

-Author Unknown

"If the claws didn't retract, cats would be like Velcro."

-*Bruce Fogle*

"If there were to be a universal sound depicting peace, I would surel
vote for the purr."

-*Barbara L. Diamond*

"Most beds sleep up to six cats. Ten cats without the owner."

-*Stephen Baker*

"My husband said it was him or the cat... I miss him sometimes."

-*Anonymous*

"I wish I could write as mysterious as a cat."

-*Edgar Allan Poe*

"I gave my cat a bath the other day... he loved it. He sat there, he enjoyed
it, it was fun for me. The fur would stick to my tongue, but other than
that."

-*Steve Martin*

"One cat just leads to another."

-*Ernest Hemingway (author)*

AUTHOR'S NOTE

We all love cats, this much is clear! Hopefully you have enjoyed reading this book as much as I have enjoyed writing it. If so I would be ever so grateful if you could take the time to leave a review on Amazon or Good reads

You may also like:

101 fun things to do in retirement: An irreverent, outrageous and fun guide to life after work – Stella Rheingold

FROM THE PUBLISHER

We take great pleasure in inviting you to join "The Sovereign Reader's Club". As a member you will get a host of special offers, from pre release advance copies of new books, FREE and discount books from the publisher, as well as the chance to give feedback and interact with your favourite authors.

http://bit.ly/1jWbqDj

Vist the above URL to sign up and receive your special joining gift of a free copy of "Think Happy: 7 Simple Steps to a Happier Life" by Margaret Hart.

58716316R00080

Made in the USA
San Bernardino, CA
29 November 2017